WORLD IN CRISIS

THE RACE TO FIND ENERGY

Nick Hunter

rosen publishing's
rosen central

NEW YORK

Published in 2015 by The Rosen Publishing Group, Inc.
29 East 21st Street
New York, NY 10010

Produced for Rosen by Calcium Creative Ltd.
Editor for Calcium Creative Ltd.: Sarah Eason
Designer: Paul Myerscough
Picture research: Rachel Blount

Library of Congress Cataloging-in-Publication Data

Hunter, Nick.
The race to find energy/by Nick Hunter.
    pages cm.—(World in crisis)
Audience: Grades 7 to 12.
Includes bibliographical references and index.
ISBN 978-1-4777-7842-5 (library bound)
1. Power resources—Juvenile literature. 2. Renewable energy sources—
Juvenile literature. I. Title.
HD9502.A2H948 2014
333.79—dc23

2013051219

Manufactured in Malaysia

Contents

The Thirst for Energy

If you could travel back in time 150 years, you would find a very different world. Most transportation relied on horsepower. The latest inventions were steam trains and ships powered by burning coal, and the first railroad to cross the United States was under construction. Homes were heated by wood or coal fires, and lit by the flickering flames of candles and whale-oil lamps. The era of heat and light at the flick of a switch, or everyday travel by car and aircraft, was still a long way off.

▲ In the nineteenth century, coal-powered steam trains enabled people to travel faster and farther than ever before.

Oil Joins the Energy Rush

For hundreds of years, people had used natural sources, including coal and wood, to provide them with energy. However, new coal-using industries and technologies, such as steam trains and the iron and steel industry, meant that the need for coal was growing fast. Coal would soon be joined by oil to deliver people's two most important fuels. The demand for oil grew at the end of the nineteenth century when automobiles, which relied on the fuel, first appeared.

Unstoppable Growth

Today, we use energy almost without thinking. The tools we use, from air-conditioning units to the phones in our pockets, are constantly burning energy. In the past 200 years, the amount of energy each person on Earth uses has increased by eight times, and there are now six times as many people on Earth as there were 200 years ago. The growth in energy use has been most dramatic since the end of World War II in 1945. Finding new sources of energy has become a vast industry. Our thirst for energy has also damaged wildlife and the planet we live on. Many scientists believe that the impact of our energy consumption could even threaten the survival of the human race itself.

COUNTDOWN!

The Energy Information Administration (EIA), part of the United States Department of Energy, predicts that the world's energy needs will increase by 56 percent between 2010 and 2040. Most of the growth in energy use will come from countries where industries are growing fast, such as China, India, and Brazil. Will we find the energy sources to meet this demand?

Modern cities rely on a constant supply of electricity for heat and light, and oil products for transportation.

CHAPTER ONE

The Clock Is Ticking

The availability of convenient sources of energy has brought many benefits to people, particularly in developed countries such as the United States and Canada. Almost every aspect of our lives, from the things we buy to the way we travel, has been transformed. However, this revolution has come at a price. As our energy use increases, the problems it causes are also increasing.

The Costs of Fuel

There are many sources of energy. Each of these sources has its benefits and drawbacks. Currently, more than 80 percent of all the world's energy supply comes from the three main fossil fuels: oil, natural gas, and coal. These fossil fuels—the compacted buried remains of living things dating back hundreds of millions of years—are often costly and dangerous to dig or drill out of the ground. They also have hidden costs such as pollution and are believed by many to be causing Earth's climate to change.

Our reliance on fossil fuels is worrying. Just a small interruption to the supply of gas can cause lines like this at gas stations.

Uses of Energy

The three biggest uses of energy are:

Power generation—every time you flick a switch in your home or school, or switch on the TV, you expect it to work instantly. Ensuring that electricity is available in every home is a huge industry. Around two-thirds of the world's electricity is generated using fossil fuels.

Transportation—there are more than one billion vehicles on the world's roads. Almost all of them are fueled by oil products, as are the thousands of aircraft and ships that cross the world every day.

Industry—energy is used to make all the things we buy, from food to footballs. Many products, such as plastics, are made from materials that are based on oil. Many of the goods we buy in stores are made in countries such as China. These goods have to be transported by ship or aircraft to customers in North America and elsewhere.

LOOK TO THE PAST

The United States and other Western countries were given a painful lesson in 1973 in how much they relied on oil. The Organization of Petroleum Exporting Countries (OPEC) is made up of many of the world's largest oil producers, particularly from the Middle East region. In 1973, the OPEC countries raised global oil prices and stopped supplying oil to the United States. Their actions had a dramatic effect on the economies of many countries as costs rose and precious oil became scarce. The crisis also prompted countries to search for other energy sources.

Running Out of Gas?

One of the reasons why our reliance on coal, oil, and natural gas is such a problem is the possibility that one day these fuels will run out. Although natural processes have created them, fossil fuels are nonrenewable sources of energy. Nonrenewable means that, once the fuels have been used, they cannot be replaced. Vital reserves of fossil fuels are also distributed unevenly around the world, meaning that the countries using the most fuel have to rely on other countries to supply their needs.

Coal is still a plentiful source of energy. Some coalmines are deep underground but large deposits can also be found close to the surface.

Fuel Buried By Nature

The name fossil fuel comes from the way these energy sources are formed. Oil and gas are made from the remains of tiny microscopic living things that have been buried over millions of years beneath layers of rock and sand. These two fuels are often found together. The remains of prehistoric trees and plants have compressed and hardened to form coal. We cannot create more of these fuels, so we depend on finding new deposits of them.

Energy Security

Fossil fuels need particular rock structures and other conditions to form, so they are not found everywhere around the world. In fact, some of the largest reserves are found in countries that have suffered from recent conflict and unstable governments, such as Iraq and Libya. Two of the world's largest producers of natural gas, Russia and Iran, have often opposed the policies of the United States and other Western nations. These countries can use the supply of oil as a weapon by threatening to cut supplies to countries they disagree with. For this reason, countries that use a lot of fossil fuels, including the United States and countries of the European Union, are keen to find sources of energy that they can control more easily.

COUNTDOWN!

No one can be sure how much oil is still under the ground. In 2007, the International Energy Agency estimated that we have used around half of the known reserves of oil. However, new discoveries of oil are being made all the time. Oil is likely to get more expensive, even if we ignore the threat of pollution and climate change.

Pollution

In October 2013, schools, roads, and the airport in the Chinese city of Harbin were closed. The city was cloaked in thick clouds of smog that meant people could see nothing more than 160 feet (50 meters) away. The burning of fossil fuels for industry and heating buildings had caused the smog. There were fears that the choking fumes could damage residents' health and bring their city to a standstill.

Danger in the Air

Harbin's smog emergency is an extreme example of the air pollution that affects many cities around the world at different times. Fumes from vehicles and factories fill the air with tiny particles that can be dangerous for human health, particularly for people who suffer from asthma and similar breathing conditions. Fumes from power plants burning coal can mix with water in the air to form acid rain. Acid rain has damaged natural habitats, including forests, and the animals and plants that live there.

Air pollution is a serious problem in some cities. Gridlocked traffic and clouds of fumes choke China's capital, Beijing.

Clean-up workers attempt to suck up the oil after an oil spill hit the coast of Thailand. Oil spills such as this cause significant long-term damage to the environment.

Oil Accidents

Energy sources do not pollute only the air. Oil has to be transported by pipeline or ship from the place where it is mined to the point where it will be refined, or separated, into oil products and then used. Leaks from pipelines or small spillages into rivers can have disastrous effects on wildlife. There have also been many instances of oil tankers being wrecked at sea, or accidents in underwater oil wells, leading to massive releases of oil into the ocean. These can have a terrible impact on wildlife over a large area. The oil spill from the ship *Exxon Valdez* in 1989 is estimated to have killed 250,000 seabirds in the delicate coastal environment of Alaska. Scientists are still assessing the cost of the vast oil spill from the Deepwater Horizon offshore oil rig, which took place in the Gulf of Mexico in 2010.

SCIENCE SOLUTIONS

Cleaning Gel

Scientists are always looking for new ways to clean up oil spills. These spills can be catastrophic for wildlife, and can also lead to the loss of large quantities of valuable oil. One group of researchers has discovered a gel that can absorb 40 times its own weight in oil. The gel can be scooped off the surface of the ocean and then refined to release the oil that the gel has absorbed. Scientists have also developed sponges that soak up oil, but not water.

From space, our atmosphere looks like a thin blue line around Earth, but without it no living thing could survive.

Climate Change

Pollution can be a major problem for people and wildlife in some regions. However, the greatest long-term danger for everyone from our reliance on fossil fuels for energy comes from climate change. Almost all scientists believe that Earth's climate is getting warmer and that this is a direct result of the massive increase in emissions of certain gases from the burning of coal, oil, and natural gas over the past 200 years.

Global Warming

The atmosphere that surrounds our planet is the essential life-support system for all living things on Earth. It contains the oxygen we need to breathe, protects us from the Sun's energy, and uses that energy to drive the weather systems that enable us to grow crops. The atmosphere contains small amounts of greenhouse gases such as carbon dioxide, which act like a blanket to keep some of the Sun's energy within the atmosphere. This is called the "greenhouse effect" and it keeps Earth's surface warm enough to support life. However, all these elements are in a very delicate balance.

Burning fossil fuels releases carbon dioxide into the atmosphere and changes the delicate balance of gases that we rely on. More of the Sun's energy is trapped. This warms the air, oceans, and land. The effects of this are complex and hard to predict, although scientists have intricate computer models that forecast what will happen under various conditions, such as if the vast ice sheets in Earth's polar regions melt.

Dangerous Experiment

By burning more and more fossil fuels and pumping more carbon dioxide into the atmosphere, we are using our planet as a giant experiment. Most experts predict that, if we continue with this experiment, it will not end well for humans or the thousands of other animal and plant species with which we share our planet.

COUNTDOWN!

In 2013, the Intergovernmental Panel on Climate Change (IPCC)—an international scientific body—released its latest report on the impact of climate change. The report predicted a temperature rise of 3 to 8° Fahrenheit (1.5 to 4.5° Celsius) by the end of this century, depending on whether we reduce our emissions of carbon dioxide gas. This could make many parts of our planet uninhabitable and could lead to a rise in sea levels of up to 32 inches (82 centimeters).

CHAPTER TWO

The Race for Fossil Fuels

Although scientists and international bodies warn us about the dangers of relying on fossil fuels, those fuels continue to supply most of the world's energy needs, and their use is still increasing. The search for new reserves of oil and gas, in particular, is carried out by some of the world's largest companies, using cutting-edge technology.

An Ever-increasing Demand

During the twentieth century, new oil fields were regularly discovered, including enormous reservoirs such as the Ghawar oil field in Saudi Arabia. That oil field alone produces more than 5 million barrels of oil every day and has produced more than 55 billion barrels in total to date. However, the world's constant thirst for energy means that even the biggest oil fields will eventually start to run dry.

Oil workers often face extreme weather conditions, including severe storms, when searching for oil beneath the ocean.

This oil pipeline crosses the frozen terrain of Alaska. It carries oil hundreds of miles across the landscape from the rich Alaskan reserves to oil refineries.

New Fuel Sources

The success of any oil company depends on being able to find new reserves. The abundant oil of the Middle East was often relatively easy to find because it lay beneath largely empty desert sands. Today, the search for oil continues in more difficult terrain, such as the frozen wastes of the Arctic, Siberia in Russia, or miles beneath the seabed. These wild frontiers of oil exploration bring new dangers and controversies. Just as controversial are other unconventional sources of oil and gas, such as oil sands—loose sands or sandstone that contain a sticky form of oil, called bitumen, or tar. In recent years, these new sources have revolutionized the shape of the oil industry, particularly in North America.

SCIENCE SOLUTIONS

Seismic Surveys

Sinking an oil well is a very expensive business, particularly in the deep ocean or a remote wilderness. Oil geologists use seismic surveys—analyses of sound waves traveling through Earth—to create a detailed map of the underground rocks where they believe they will find oil. Electric pulses are fired into the ground to try to determine the structure of rocks. Massive computer systems then process the resulting data to create a picture of possible oil reserves. Accurate mapping can mean the difference between a multibillion-dollar oil strike and a costly dry well.

Thousands of workers worked to deal with aftermath of the Deepwater Horizon oil spill. The effect of the spill on wildlife and the surrounding landscape was devastating.

Going Deeper and Wilder

On April 20, 2010, an explosion shattered the Deepwater Horizon oil rig in the Gulf of Mexico. The blast killed 11 oil workers and injured many more. On the seabed, 5,000 ft (1,520 m) below, crude oil began to gush into the ocean. According to official estimates, over the following weeks, as engineers struggled to control the leak, 4.9 million barrels of oil leaked into the Gulf, creating the biggest peacetime oil spill in history.

Deepwater Risks

The Deepwater Horizon disaster was a dramatic demonstration of the dangers of drilling for oil in deep water. Oil exploration at sea is not a recent development, but advances in technology now make it possible for giant floating oil platforms to operate in the deepest areas of ocean. If something goes wrong a mile or more below the surface of the sea, extreme cold and water pressure make it much more difficult to fix. The demand for oil, and high oil prices, mean that oil companies are willing to take the risk and pay the huge costs of pushing into new frontiers for oil exploration. Oil companies are now exploiting deepwater oil reserves in many parts of the world, including off the coasts of Brazil and Nigeria.

The hunt for oil and gas also happens in some of the most extreme environments on Earth, such as the icy waters of the Arctic Ocean. Arctic exploration is now made possible because the area covered by ice sheets is shrinking due to climate change. Those who oppose Arctic oil point out that these delicate regions, which are not exposed to the Sun for much of the year, could be damaged forever by oil exploration.

The Human Cost

People can also be affected by the oil industry. For example, people of the Niger Delta in Nigeria have claimed that the land they farm for food has been contaminated by repeated oil spills. Their homes and livelihood are under threat, but they see none of the financial benefit from the valuable oil beneath their land.

SCIENCE SOLUTIONS

Arctic Risks

Drilling for oil in the Arctic carries huge risks. The Arctic Ocean is covered with ice for much of the year, and oil companies have almost no experience of dealing with an oil spill beneath the ice. New technologies, including unmanned drone aircraft and remotely operated underwater vehicles, are being tested to deal with a possible disaster in the Arctic.

The coastline of Louisiana, shown here covered in oil from a spill, is a habitat for birds and other animals.

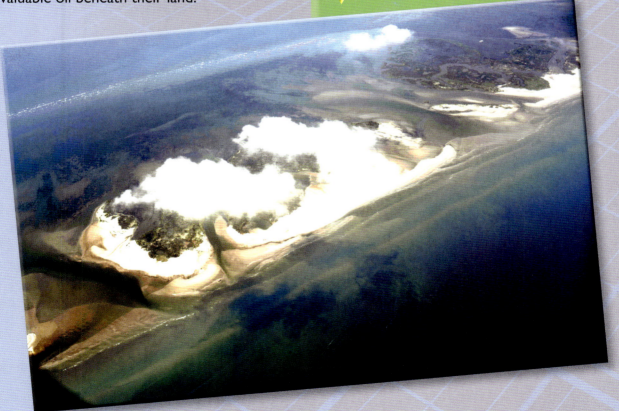

Unconventional Oil and Gas

The search for new sources of oil and gas is relentless. Recently, oil companies have developed ways of extracting oil that they had previously considered too difficult or expensive. Particularly in North America, these new techniques have increased the amount of oil and gas that can be produced closer to home. This has helped to reduce reliance on fuel imports from the giant oil fields of the Middle East.

Oil Sands

All oil is not alike. Light crude oil can be extracted by drilling down into reservoirs and allowing pressure to force it up to the surface. Some oil, such as the deposits found in the oil sands of Canada and Venezuela, is in the form of sticky tar. It cannot be refined into gasoline and the many other products that come from crude oil until it has been heated and treated to convert it into a liquid. High oil prices and a lack of other major oil discoveries have convinced oil companies that this costly and energy-hungry process is worthwhile.

Protestors campaign against fracking, and the damage they say it causes to the water supplies in nearby areas.

Oil is extracted from oil sands in Alberta, Canada. These rich reserves supply oil to much of North America.

Opponents say that the exploitation of oil sands is environmental vandalism. They say that the energy needed to make this oil usable is contributing even more to the problems of climate change when, instead, we need to be looking for solutions.

Shale Gas

The technique of hydraulic fracturing, or fracking, has been used to release large quantities of gas from layers of impermeable shale rock. A mixture of water, sand, and other chemicals is fired into the rock at high pressure, fracturing the layers of rock and releasing the gas. The fracking process uses a lot of water and energy to extract the gas, and opponents are concerned that chemicals could contaminate the surrounding water supplies that farmers and residents rely on. It has even been claimed that fracking is responsible for creating small earthquakes.

LOOK TO THE PAST

Heavy oil, or bitumen, such as that extracted from oil sands, is not a new discovery. The ancient Egyptians used bitumen for preserving mummies. Its water-resistant properties made bitumen useful for many tasks, from sealing the planks on wooden sailing ships to creating road surfaces in the nineteenth century.

Cleaner Fossil Fuels

In spite of everything we know about the damage that fossil fuels do to our environment, they still provide most of the world's energy and their use is growing every year. While campaigners call for the world to switch to other energy sources, we also need to find ways to limit the damage caused by fossil fuels.

Is Gas the Answer?

The growth in use of natural gas for generating power, cooking, and heating has been a major change in recent decades. Gas releases 30 percent less carbon dioxide than oil when burned, and 45 percent less than coal. Even so, 5 percent of the gas that comes out of the ground is burned or flared off immediately rather than used, because it is sometimes seen as an unwanted by-product of oil production.

One of the biggest drawbacks of gas is that it is more expensive to transport than oil or coal. This is not a big problem if gas can be transported by pipeline, but gas that is transported by ship has to be cooled into liquid form and converted into gas again at its destination.

▲ Gas is often burned off during oil drilling because it is more difficult to transport than other fossil fuels such as coal or oil. .

Cleaner Cars

Although liquefied natural gas (LNG) is used as a cleaner type of fuel in some vehicles, most of the vehicles on the world's roads are powered by gasoline or diesel. Hybrid vehicles use an electric motor alongside a regular gasoline-powered engine to make cars more efficient. High oil prices have persuaded many drivers to look for cars that use less fuel, so hybrid cars are gradually becoming a more popular choice. The growth of cleaner cars will be important as car ownership spreads in countries with high populations such as China and India.

Many hybrid cars run mostly on electricity, with a gasoline engine as a backup. Will charging points like this soon be a common sight in cities?

SCIENCE SOLUTIONS

Capturing Carbon

Coal is still used in power generation in many countries, particularly in the industrial superpower China. Many of China's new coal-fired power stations use technology to make them more efficient and to prevent emissions of gases that cause acid rain. Scientists are also working on ways to capture the harmful carbon dioxide released when coal is burned. One process, known as carbon capture and storage (CCS), can either separate the carbon dioxide from coal before it is burned, or capture the gas after the coal is burned. CCS has been tried on a small scale, but making it universal would require around 350,000 miles (563,000 kilometers) of pipelines in the United States alone.

CHAPTER THREE

Energy from the Atom

In the 1950s, the acute energy crisis the world faces now was still a long way off, with the science of climate change in its infancy. As the world recovered from World War II, scientists thought they had found the answer to future energy needs. Nuclear power released by the splitting of uranium atoms would provide clean and plentiful energy to replace coal and oil. By 2012, there were more than 400 nuclear reactors in 30 countries, but the future of nuclear power now is far from certain.

The Spread of Nuclear Power

The first commercial nuclear reactor started operating at Calder Hall, in the United Kingdom, in 1956. Nuclear power spread rapidly, particularly as the oil crises of the 1970s convinced governments that they should generate their own electricity. The United States is home to more than 100 nuclear power plants, with Japan and European countries such as France also having invested in nuclear power. Small nuclear reactors are even used to power warships and submarines, ensuring that they never need to refuel as they travel.

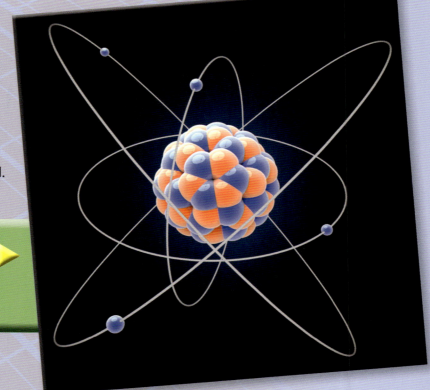

Breaking the bonds that hold the center, or nucleus, of an atom together releases a lot of energy.

How Nuclear Power Works

Strong forces hold atoms together. Nuclear power uses the energy released when atoms are split and those bonds are broken to heat water into steam. This steam drives big engines, called turbines, to produce electricity. Nuclear power does not produce the fumes or greenhouse gases released by coal-fired power stations.

However, despite its many benefits, nuclear power produced only 11 percent of the world's electricity in 2011, which was less than the 17 percent produced at its peak in 1993. The clean nuclear future that was once promised has clearly not happened.

The cost and public concerns about safety mean that many countries are reluctant to build new nuclear power stations.

LOOK TO THE PAST

When the world took its first steps in nuclear power during the 1950s, there were claims that this new source of energy would dramatically reduce the cost of electricity so that it would become "too cheap to meter." Unfortunately, things were not as simple as that. Safety considerations and the cost of technology have meant that nuclear power plants are very costly to build. Reactors do not last forever and have to be replaced after about 40 years.

This area is closed because of radiation from the Fukushima disaster. It is more than 130 miles (210 km) away and the radiation is thought to come from rainwater.

Nuclear Drawbacks

On March 11, 2011, a violent tsunami hit the east coast of Japan, following an earthquake beneath the Pacific Ocean. The Fukushima nuclear power plant was directly in the path of the giant wave, which caused cooling systems to fail. In one of the world's worst nuclear accidents, fuel rods overheated and, along with huge explosions, harmful radiation escaped from the power plant.

Following the disaster, 47,000 residents were evacuated from homes within 19 miles (30 km) of the stricken reactors. People in the areas affected worst will not be able to return to their homes before 2017, when contaminated topsoil and vegetation have been removed. Many people have decided never to return to the area.

Weighing Up the Risks

The accident at Fukushima reminded the world that nuclear power is far from being a risk-free solution to our energy worries. It was the latest in a series of nuclear accidents that had affected the industry. Nuclear fuel is able to release enormous amounts of energy, but the reactions inside a nuclear power plant can quickly get out of control when things go wrong. Many countries have reassessed nuclear power and canceled plans to invest in new nuclear reactors since the Fukushima incident.

For and Against

Supporters of nuclear power argue that accidents are rare, and that the risks of climate change are far greater in the long term. Opponents of nuclear power point out that, although nuclear power produces a tiny amount of waste when compared to coal-fired power stations, this waste is hazardous to transport and store. There are also concerns that nuclear power plants could be targets for terrorists, or that nuclear material suitable for making a weapon could fall into the wrong hands. Are there any ways that the nuclear industry can overcome these dangers and drawbacks?

COUNTDOWN!

The used fuel from nuclear reactors remains dangerous after it is removed from the reactor. Uranium atoms continue to decay, releasing radiation that can damage the human body and other living things if they come into contact with it. Most waste will remain hazardous for decades, and some of the most hazardous waste needs to be stored for thousands of years before it is safe.

Nuclear power uses the same technology used to create nuclear weapons. Many people are concerned that nuclear fuel could be obtained and used by terrorist groups.

Nuclear Fusion

Scientists continue to make nuclear reactors more efficient and safe. However, the best option for the future of nuclear power may be nuclear fusion, a process in which atoms release energy as they are fused together, rather than as they split apart—the opposite process, called fission. Nuclear fusion is also the process that takes place at the heart of the Sun, releasing the energy that lights and heats our planet.

The advantage of nuclear fusion over conventional nuclear power is that when atoms fuse together there is no harmful radioactive waste to be disposed of. It is also unlikely that scientists would lose control of a fusion reaction in the way they have done in past nuclear fission accidents.

Controlling Fusion

Scientists have already achieved nuclear fusion in the awesome destructive power of the hydrogen bomb, the most powerful weapon on Earth. However, to make nuclear fusion useful as a source of energy, they need to be able to control the process. That is much more difficult. To begin with, the energy released would destroy any conventional container. A possible solution to this problem is to contain that immense energy within a powerful magnetic field.

World Search for Fusion

The quest for nuclear fusion is a rare project for which the governments of the world have come together, hoping to find a solution to our energy crisis.

This device, called a tokamak, will one day hold the fusion reaction in place using a magnetic field. Any material container would be destroyed by the heat of the reaction.

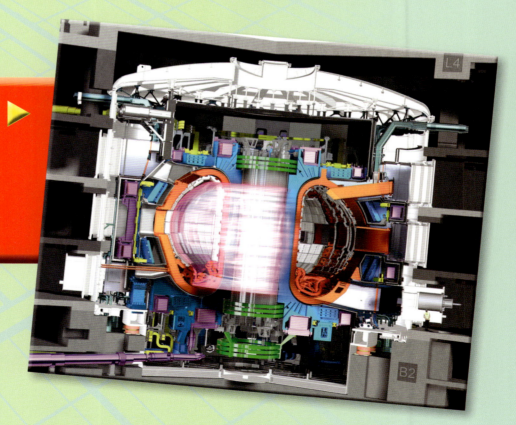

Thirty-four governments, representing more than half of the world's population, have poured billions of dollars into developing an experimental nuclear fusion reactor in southern France, called the ITER project. The reactor is built of more than one million components from around the world. However, the first fusion reaction of the ITER project is unlikely to take place before 2030.

This is the building site for the ITER nuclear fusion reactor in southern France. It is hoped the plant will deliver some solution to France's energy crisis.

SCIENCE SOLUTIONS

Fusion Breakthrough

In 2013, scientists at the National Ignition Facility in California reported a breakthrough in the pursuit of nuclear fusion. By focusing 192 of the world's most powerful lasers on to a tiny piece of hydrogen fuel, they had succeeded in creating a fusion reaction that produced more energy than was actually reaching the fuel. Although power generated by controlled nuclear fusion is still a long way off, scientists believe this breakthrough is a crucial milestone on the way to achieving their goal.

CHAPTER FOUR

Energy Alternatives

There are big drawbacks in using fossil fuels and nuclear power to provide the energy we need. Around 13 percent of the world's energy supply comes from alternative sources, although this figure largely refers to wood and other materials burned for heat and cooking by the millions of people who do not have access to energy supplies such as coal, oil, and gas.

Using the Sun

The ultimate source of most energy on Earth is the Sun, and the massive nuclear fusion reactions that take place at its center. In addition to providing warmth, the Sun's energy drives winds and weather systems. It powers the water cycle that feeds our rivers, and heats and waters plants and other living things. All of these can be used as sources of energy, but they currently make up only a tiny part of our energy supply. Unlike fossil fuels, these alternative energy sources are renewable—they will never run out as long as the Sun keeps shining.

The Sun is expected to keep burning for another 5 billion years, so the Sun at least is one source of energy that will not run out.

Fighting for the Alternatives

Alternative energy sources have the potential to provide clean, safe energy that could reduce our reliance on fossil fuels, but each of them has limitations that must be overcome. Across the world, scientists and engineers are working hard to find solutions to these limitations.

Alternative energy sources also have to gain a foothold in a well-established energy world that is difficult to change. A network of gas stations serves the drivers of motor vehicles, so they can easily fill them with fuel. Power plants using nuclear energy and fossil fuels are costly to build and cannot quickly be replaced by alternative fuel sources. Despite these obstacles, energy alternatives will need to be a bigger part of the energy mix in the future.

LOOK TO THE PAST

Before the use of fossil fuels became widespread, clean alternative energy sources were the only option. Mills used the power of the wind or flowing water to turn the heavy stone wheels that ground wheat to make flour. Ships also used the wind to carry them across the ocean.

Capturing the Sun's Energy

The Sun provides us with an almost infinite source of energy. It causes no carbon dioxide emissions, but less than one-thousandth of the energy we use comes directly from the Sun. Why are we not making more use of solar energy?

Taking Advantage of the Sun

We can capture the Sun's energy using solar thermal energy or photovoltaic cells. Solar thermal energy uses the Sun's energy to heat water in pipes. Photovoltaic cells, such as the one you have on your pocket calculator, can turn the light of the Sun into electrical energy. While this works well for a device such as a calculator that requires little power, photovoltaic cells are not without problems. At present, these cells are not very efficient, meaning that only a small part of the energy received from the Sun is converted to electricity. To produce a good supply of electricity, a large area needs to be covered with photovoltaic cells.

Where the Sun Shines

The availability of sunshine is an important factor in the use of solar energy. The areas with most sunshine are usually in desert regions where few people live. The places where power is most needed are close to cities, where there is little space for large areas of photovoltaic panels. We also tend to use least energy when the Sun is shining strongly, because we need less heat and light.

The Sun's energy is often used to power spacecraft and satellites once they leave Earth's atmosphere.

This building uses solar panels over its windows to generate electricity and provide shade to the people inside.

Another big issue with solar energy is how to transport and store the electricity it generates so it is available in the right place at the right time.

Concentrated Solar Power

The latest use of solar energy is in concentrated solar power plants. These use mirrors and other techniques to focus the Sun's rays on a central point so it can heat water to make steam, which can then drive electricity turbines. Solar power towers using this process can provide electricity for thousands of homes in areas where sunshine is constant and reliable.

COUNTDOWN!

The Sun gives out more energy in a single second than the United States uses in an entire year. Only a small part of that energy reaches Earth, but a single day's sunshine could meet our energy needs for many years if we could harness it. The Sun has been burning for around 5 billion years and is only about halfway through its lifetime.

Wind turbines are most useful in countries where winds blow strongly and predictably, such as around northern coasts of Europe.

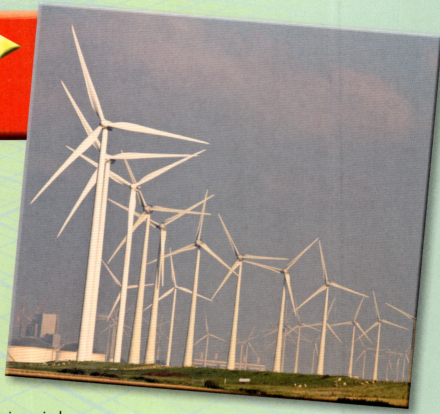

Water, Waves, and Wind

Water and wind have been used for thousands of years as sources of energy, from the time when the first travelers used a sail to capture the energy to move a boat. Today, wind and water are the most successful alternative energy sources. Some European nations generate more than 15 percent of their electricity using wind power. Energy from water may provide just over 2 percent of the world's power supply, but it delivers a much higher share of electricity generation in many individual countries. The biggest nations, such as United States and China, are catching up fast, so maybe these clean sources can solve the world's energy problems.

Wind Power

Energy can be created easily using wind turbines, which work like giant windmills. Bigger turbines work more effectively than small ones, and the tallest can be more than 600 ft (180 m) high. The main drawback of wind energy is that it takes many turbines to match the output of one gas-fired power plant.

Water Power

Water has been used to generate electricity for many decades. Dams—large barriers built across rivers or lakes—harness the power of water flowing downhill by funneling it through turbines that produce electricity. This is very effective in mountainous countries with fast-flowing rivers. The biggest problem with these huge projects is the effect they can have on wildlife and people living close to the river. Valleys upstream are flooded to contain the water held back by the dam, meaning that people and animals have to move or be drowned. Areas downstream of the dam experience a reduced flow of water that can be just as damaging.

The awesome power of the oceans could also provide more energy in future. Several projects are under way to build turbines that can capture the unpredictable energy of ocean waves, and withstand the constant battering of the seas.

SCIENCE SOLUTIONS

Turning the Tide

Unlike waves and wind, tidal flows are regular and predictable. Tidal barrages—damlike barriers built across bays or river mouths—can capture the energy of these massive water flows. One of the most successful tidal barrages is in the Bay of Fundy in Canada. Supporters of a proposed barrage across the Severn Estuary in Britain claim it could provide enough power for 3 million people. However, the costs of around $40 billion and the possible damage to wildlife have stopped the project moving forward.

The giant Three Gorges dam in China was controversial because its construction flooded a river valley, including several villages.

Biomass and Biofuels

Biomass is material that comes from living or recently living things, such as trees, plants, and farm waste, which can be burned for heating and cooking. It accounts for around one-tenth of the world's energy supply, although most of this is in the developing countries of Africa and South Asia, where millions of people have no direct access to electricity or fossil fuels. Biomass is only slightly cleaner than coal, but the use of plants and similar materials as a source of alternative energy could challenge fossil fuels.

Biofuels, such as bioethanol and biodiesel, are liquid fuels that can be made from plants. The great advantage of biofuels is that they can be used in vehicles, usually when mixed with gasoline or diesel. Biodiesel is made from oilseeds, such as rapeseed, and can be used on its own as a fuel for some diesel vehicles. Although biofuel crops release carbon dioxide when they are burned, all plants absorb carbon dioxide as they grow, so the overall effect is balanced.

The Trouble with Biofuels

If biofuels were to replace fossil fuels altogether in vehicles, huge areas of land would have to be given over to growing the crops needed to make biofuels. This would involve cutting down most of the world's forests. Forests take in carbon dioxide from the atmosphere. They have a vital role to play in combating climate change, so losing the forests would make the situation worse rather than better.

Palm oil is used in biodiesel, but these crops have a big environmental impact as rain forests and other habitats are cut down to make room for them.

In many areas, forests are already being cut down to grow biofuel crops such as soybeans and oil palm trees. These crops are also taking land that was previously used to grow food. This leads to a rise in food prices, which affects all of us but especially the world's poorest people, who cannot afford increases in their cost of living.

Amazing Algae

The next generation of biofuels, such as algae, could solve some of these problems. Algae are tiny plants that can be grown in water and then used to make biofuels. While they are growing, they soak up harmful carbon dioxide from the water.

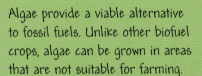
Algae provide a viable alternative to fossil fuels. Unlike other biofuel crops, algae can be grown in areas that are not suitable for farming.

SCIENCE SOLUTIONS

Waste to Fuel

Turning plant waste from farming into fuel might be an attractive solution to our energy problems. Scientists have developed a special form of yeast that can break down plant waste, such as straw, to create fuel. This may mean that biofuels could be created from the same plants that are also providing us with food.

Geothermal Energy

If you have ever seen pictures of a volcano erupting, you will know about the enormous heat and energy that sits deep below Earth's surface. Beneath Earth's crust lies more than 70,000 times the energy that is available from fossil fuels. The temperature at Earth's core is around 8,000°F (4,400°C), and this heat is pushed up to the surface, where it bursts through in the form of volcanoes and hot springs. This is known as geothermal energy.

Geothermal energy is available everywhere, but it is most often used in areas that have a great deal of volcanic activity, such as Iceland. Almost all of the domestic heating in Iceland's capital, Reykjavik, is provided by geothermal energy. More than 78 countries use geothermal energy in some form, but it is usually only a small part of the energy mix.

Geothermal energy means that Iceland's homes can be warmed with almost no use of fossil fuels.

The Potential of Geothermal

The power of geothermal energy can be used very simply to provide heating. Water that has been heated underground is fed through pipes and radiators. Underground energy can also be used to generate electricity, although only 0.25 percent of the world's electricity is produced in this way. The United States Department of Energy believes that 10 percent of U.S. energy needs could be met with geothermal energy in the future. The main obstacle is the high cost of building geothermal power plants.

Heat Pumps

You do not have to drill down deep into Earth's crust to find geothermal energy. The temperature of the air and buildings above ground may change substantially between summer and winter, but a few feet below the surface the temperature remains fairly constant. Geothermal, or ground source, heat pumps can access this energy using pipes laid beneath the ground. Water or other fluid in the pipes is heated by the constant underground temperature and can be used to push warm air into a building, or remove it, to keep that building warm in winter and cool in summer.

Geothermal power plants are costly to build, but the huge advantage of this energy form is that it is unlikely to run out.

LOOK TO THE PAST

Geothermal energy has been used for thousands of years in places where it is easy to access. In ancient times, Native Americans used geothermal energy for cooking. The people of the Roman city of Pompeii used energy from beneath the ground to heat their baths. Unfortunately, there was too much geothermal activity around Pompeii, and the town was buried after a volcanic eruption in 79 AD.

CHAPTER FIVE

Future Solutions

There is already a wide range of energy sources that could provide us with clean, renewable energy for the future. However, they all have some drawbacks. Scientists are working to try to find solutions to these issues, and to discover new sources of energy that will provide even better alternatives to fossil fuels.

Ocean Energy

The water in the oceans may not feel very warm sometimes, but water near the surface effectively stores much of the energy we receive from the Sun. Using a process called ocean thermal energy conversion, this warm water can create steam to drive electricity turbines. The water is then cooled using cold water from the ocean depths.

Oil Substitute

Some experts believe that the future of energy is to make more oil. The water-borne plants called algae are being used to create a kind of green fuel oil, which can

This experimental aircraft is fueled by algae-based biofuel. Could all our aircraft one day be fueled by this energy source?

be processed into products such as aviation fuel. The algae also absorb carbon dioxide as they are grown. Other carbon-based wastes, such as leftover foods and old tires, can also be converted into oil-like substances. However, these processes require energy themselves and do little to tackle the fundamental causes of climate change.

Human Power

The answer to some of our energy needs could be our own bodies. We eat food to give us energy. Some of us then go to the gym or ride a bicycle to get rid of excess energy. Researchers are currently investigating ways to harness the energy we expend on treadmills or exercise bikes to make electricity.

Gas from Trash

We could use the energy that is released when the trash we throw away decays in landfills. Researchers in the United States have developed a system that turns trash into pellets and then into a clean synthetic gas that can be used to drive an electricity generator.

SCIENCE SOLUTIONS

Natural Cooling

Along with finding new energy sources, we should also be trying to use less energy where we live and work. Roof gardens can provide insulation to keep buildings cool in summer and warm in winter. Newer buildings can include natural cooling systems to remove the need for expensive air conditioning.

Hydrogen is an abundant energy source that fuels the Sun. Could it also provide a solution to our energy problems?

Hydrogen Fuel Cells

One of the big problems with alternative energy sources such as solar energy is that they are difficult to store. Hydrogen fuel cells could be used as a way of storing and transporting energy to where it is needed. The gas hydrogen is the most abundant substance in our solar system. It is the fuel for the fusion reactions that take place inside the Sun. On Earth, the gas combines with oxygen to make the water that is essential for all living things. Hydrogen is also present with carbon in fossil fuels. Many experts believe that hydrogen itself should play a bigger part in our energy future.

To be useful as a fuel, hydrogen has to be separated from other substances, using energy. Once it has been separated it can be stored. Hydrogen fuel cells use hydrogen and oxygen to produce energy.

The only by-product of this process is water. These fuel cells could be the solution for the clean vehicles of the future.

The Problem with Hydrogen

If the technology already exists, why do we not see hydrogen cars on the road every day? Refueling is the main problem. Traditional gasoline-fueled cars can use a gas station. Hybrid and electric cars can be plugged in overnight, and electric charging points are fairly easy to install. Hydrogen, however, is explosive, so requires a network of special pipelines and storage. This network will not be built until people start driving hydrogen cars, but there is no point in having a hydrogen car in the first place if you cannot refuel it.

Challenges to Hydrogen

Despite these problems, until a few years ago hydrogen cars seemed like they would be the vehicles of the future. However, hydrogen's promise as a fuel has been hit by improvements to hybrid and electric cars. These cars are still only a small fraction of all the vehicles sold, but hybrid technologies are increasingly popular. By driving a car that combines a traditional engine with an electric motor, hybrid owners can reduce their fuel bills and cause less harm to the environment. As electric car technology develops, these vehicles could make a real difference in the fight to end reliance on fossil fuels. However, hydrogen may still have a part to play as a fuel for industrial use and for public buses that can be refueled at a central depot.

SCIENCE SOLUTIONS

Fake Fossil Fuel

All plants absorb carbon dioxide by a process called photosynthesis. Researchers at the University of California, Berkeley, have invented a way to do this artificially, using carbon dioxide, water, and sunlight to create fuels made of hydrogen and carbon, similar to fossil fuels.

Hybrid cars offer an immediate solution to the energy crisis. They use existing technologies alongside new ones and do not need a new network of refueling stations.

Can We Win the Race?

The energy needs of the world change all the time. In 1973, China used just 8 percent of the world's energy. Today, it uses around 20 percent and has overtaken the United States as the world's biggest source of carbon dioxide emissions. China's rise has also been partly responsible for a big increase in the use of coal, the world's most polluting fuel. However, the amount of carbon dioxide that China produces per person is still much lower than that of the United States.

The Slow Pace of Change

Overall, energy use is increasing, and it often seems as if the world is making no progress in the battle to switch to new sources of energy, in spite of the constant warnings from scientists about the dangers of climate change. However, changes in energy policy on a world scale are difficult to achieve. Power plants

Car production is increasing in car manufacturing plants in India and China. Millions of people in these two countries would like to own cars. This will be difficult to achieve while reducing carbon dioxide emissions.

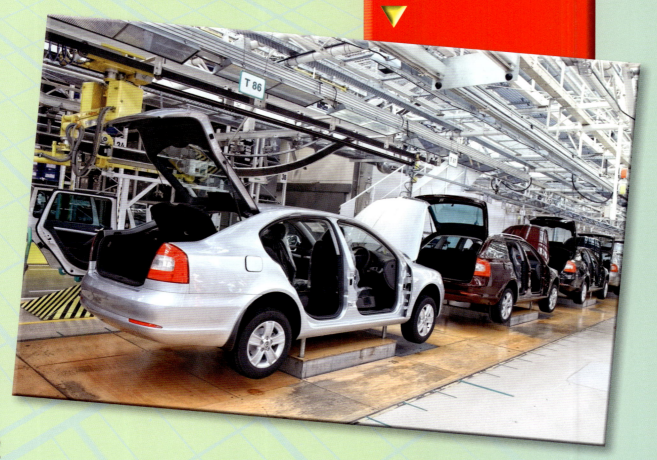

Our planet is lit up at night when viewed from space. Rising energy costs are a powerful way of persuading people to use less energy.

burning coal are easier and less expensive to build than nuclear or geothermal facilities. More energy-efficient cars and homes often cost more money. Many powerful companies and industries have good reasons to argue against a shift to renewable energy sources that would damage their own positions.

Hope for the Future

As the energy crisis becomes more urgent every year, there are some positive signs that the world can move away from fossil fuels. Many countries are investing heavily in renewable energy, including some of the Arab states that have grown rich from their reserves of oil. Consumers in Western countries have started to choose hybrid vehicles and other energy-saving measures as energy costs have risen. However, there is still a very long way to go.

LOOK TO THE PAST

The world community has overcome many challenges in the past. In the 1980s, a hole was discovered in the ozone layer high up in Earth's atmosphere. This layer provides essential protection from the Sun's harmful rays. The hole was caused mainly by gases called chlorofluorocarbons (CFCs) that were used, among other things, to force the contents out of aerosols and as a coolant in refrigerators. Almost 200 countries agreed to ban these substances. It will be many decades before the ozone layer fully recovers, but this action shows that the world community can respond to a crisis.

Extra carbon dioxide in the atmosphere is being absorbed by the oceans and threatening the marine life.

Will It Cost the Earth?

Even if the world succeeds in making the switch to energy sources that do not produce carbon dioxide, it is too late to stop all climate change. Scientists around the world are convinced that human-made climate change is already happening, due to the high levels of greenhouse gases in the atmosphere. It could take many years for Earth's climate system to readjust. However, if we can make the switch to new energy sources, there may still be time to stop the worst effects of climate change.

The Way Forward

The world's political leaders have reached some agreements on slowing climate change, but so far they have not been able to halt the rising tide of carbon dioxide emissions. Newly industrialized nations such as China and India want to enjoy the same lifestyle enjoyed by many people in developed countries such as the United States. The world must find a way of increasing living standards for billions of people while reducing carbon emissions.

What Can We Do Now?

Industries can help by producing technologies that will use less energy, or promote the use of new energy sources, while reducing costs and the amount of energy used by consumers. As individuals, it can be difficult for us to choose where our energy comes from, unless we choose green technology such as an electric vehicle. What we can do is watch carefully the amount of energy we use, and convince governments and industries to make new sources of energy a priority.

Current progress may seem slow, but experts hope that once people and industries begin to choose new energy sources, change will quickly gather pace. They hope that this energy shift will come before climate change reaches the point beyond which a major impact on our lives and our planet cannot be stopped.

Climate change is having a devastating effect on the planet's wildlife. Polar bears face losing their habitat if Arctic ice melts because of climate change.

COUNTDOWN!

The IPCC monitors the changes to our climate, which it believes are caused by human activities, particularly our use of fossil fuels. The IPCC's latest report concludes that global temperatures have risen faster over the past 100 years than ever before, and that the chemical balance of the oceans has changed as they have absorbed increasing amounts of carbon dioxide. Experts had warned that keeping the temperature rise to less than 4°F (2°C) might prevent "dangerous climate change." However, we have already emitted enough extra carbon dioxide to make this increase almost inevitable.

Glossary

acid rain Rain that has reacted with air pollution to become an acid, which can harm trees, buildings, and animals.

algae Tiny plantlike organisms that grow in water.

atmosphere The layer of gases surrounding Earth that contains the oxygen that humans and other animals need in order to breathe.

atom The smallest units or particles of matter.

biofuels Fuels made from plant material.

carbon dioxide The greenhouse gas released when fossil fuels and organic matter are burned.

climate change The theory that Earth's climate is getting warmer and that this is caused by human actions such as burning fossil fuels.

contaminate To pollute or make unclean through contact with an impure substance.

crude oil The form in which oil is taken from the ground before it is refined, or separated, to make several different substances.

developed country A wealthy industrial country where the economy is fully developed, such as the United States or Canada.

emissions The gases that are released during a process, such as the carbon dioxide released when fossil fuels are burned.

evacuate To arrange for people to leave a building or area because they are in danger.

fossil fuels The energy sources, including coal, oil, and natural gas, formed from the decayed remains of living things.

fusion A process where two things come together to form something new. In nuclear fusion, hydrogen atoms come together to create helium.

geologist A scientist who studies rocks and the make-up of Earth's crust.

geothermal Relating to heat from beneath Earth's surface.

greenhouse gas A gas that absorbs heat in the atmosphere.

habitat The place where an animal or plant usually lives.

particles Tiny pieces.

radiation The harmful particles emitted by materials used in nuclear power generation.

reactor A building in which a nuclear chain reaction can be started and controlled to provide nuclear power.

nonrenewable Energy resources that can only be used once and that do not naturally recur.

photovoltaic cell A device that converts energy from the Sun into electricity

renewable An energy source that can be used again and again, such as wind or solar power.

seismic Relating to vibrations in Earth's crust.

turbine A motor driven by air, steam, or water power that generates electricity.

Further Reading

Books

Brevard McClean, Katherine. *The Story of Oil: How It Changed the World*. North Mankato, MN: Compass Point Books, 2010.

Challoner, Jack. *Energy* (Eyewitness). New York, NY: Dorling Kindersley, 2012.

Chambers, Catherine. *Energy in Crisis* (Protecting Our Planet). New York, NY: Crabtree Publishing, 2010.

Hunter, Nick. *How Electric and Hybrid Cars Work* (Ecoworks). New York, NY: Gareth Stevens, 2013.

Hunter, Nick. *Science Vs. the Energy Crisis* (Science Fights Back). New York, NY: Gareth Stevens, 2013.

McLeish, Ewan. *The Pros and Cons of Nuclear Power* (The Energy Debate). New York, NY: Rosen Central, 2007.

Web Sites

Due to the changing nature of Internet links, Rosen Publishing has developed an online list of Web sites related to the subject of this book. This site is updated regularly. Please use this link to access the list:

http://www.rosenlinks.com/WIC/Ener

Index